Discovering Sea Glass

POEMS

By
Brian Mahoney

ISBN: 9781957863542

Cover Photo: Tina Horne, iStockphoto.com

PARISIANPHOENIX.COM

angel@parisianphoenix.com

parisianphoenixpublishing.substack.com

@parisianphoenixpublishing
/parisan-phoenix-publishing
/parisianphoenixpublishing
@parisianphoenix
/parisianphoenix.bsky.social

parisian phoenix
PUBLISHING

This book is dedicated to my wife, Kelly

"Life is like a camera. Just focus on what's important and capture the good times, develop from the negatives, and if things don't work out, just take another shot."

Table of Contents

Foreword & Introduction

"We don't read and write poetry because it's cute. We read and write poetry because we are members of the human race. And the human race is filled with passion. And medicine, law, business, engineering... these are noble pursuits and necessary to sustain life. But poetry, beauty, romance, love... these are what we stay alive for." ~ ROBIN WILLIAMS, DEAD POETS SOCIETY

I published my first book of poetry in 2011 while as an undergraduate at Kutztown University of Pennsylvania. I had a flurry of strong emotions tied to romantic struggles, college experiences, and a craving for wild expression.

I knew after graduating from the stable routines and a bustling campus town, the real world would be an unpredictable journey. It came with some rip currents, changing tides, and a deeper dive reflecting upon the complexities of my own soul.

Nearly 15 years later, this poetry book encompasses a passing of critical time: The formative years of living through the middle 20s and early 30s. This growth resonates with people profoundly—whether it's being lost in career pursuits, finding love or philosophical belonging, and the attempts of reaching self-actualization.

This book illustrates how you can develop into the person you become, shaped by circumstances or experiences— shedding light on one's own truth. With the passing of time for us—just like how sea glass is formed— there may be a broken shard of us that will encounter daunting amounts of sand, rocks, storms, and waves.

Moving back and forth within these currents, sea glass safely returns polished on land. Similarly, to how sea glass forms, we ourselves may lose some color or sharpness from being weathered. But in the end, gain a new color with a more hardened, smoother, and wholesome object waiting to be discovered.

These connected pieces found inside my writing over the years gave birth to *Discovering Sea Glass*.

Lastly—A huge thank you to Angel Ackerman for making this possible. Enjoy the book!

(July 02, 2025)

Part One

Endeavors

Every hero has a challenge.
Every good story has a twist.

Questions we wage war with
Are matches made for enkindled truth.

Crying it out slowly, laughing masks
Our autobiographic disturbance.
Curtains can move aside.

Lights flash
Once you see
This hollow realm—
Straight ahead
It's Oscar-winning warmth
Or a cold jury deciding
Your last meal.

Sentiments we feel, a voice
Felt from beneath
Drive our movements
Day and night. It's an endless
Show and tell.

Graffiti

Doodles upon concrete,
We perceive the ammo
Born out of our imagination:

Keith Haring figures dance in bliss
Shadowy girls we'd want to kiss

Peeping eyes bulge of a lad
Through a thick theatre curtain hole—
The royal smile and frown dyad
Orbits near Pennywise, dark as coal.

The Tortoise in heavy metal gear
Pushes down dynamite
Tied to the Hare in distress.

BOOM.

Band album logos blazing
Baseball wordmark fine stitching.
Old high school teachers
Made with misshapen spider legs.

Unicorns charging with natural glee
Blazing by Ukrainian flags
Flying far as the eye can see.
Neighboring token sunflowers
Tower high above
Monkeys killing queens.

Houston is set on fire.
A slick Santa sketched
To sail seven seas.
A guitar played by Jesus—
"Johnny B. Goode" in tight jeans.

"Why'd you do that?" they say to me…
In a restroom. In a grimy stairwell.

Graffiti now—breaking the rules.
Ask a stubborn Banksy.
He will declare his terms—
He needed more distance from such a Hell.

Audacious

Strip out my words,
Our so-called Standard American English.
Enough with the codes
And incinerate my tongue.

I'll incinerate it myself
Because of those dopey words,
Abysmal feelings—
I spewed them out.

Wouldn't that make you sick?
A million of us
Know quite well
When it's time to thaw ice
Holding still these veins
The special, unloved pains.

Plagiarize my worded wonderings,
Lifted eyes to a sly Buddha.
I'm brought to peace
While I shamefully search
For your Hell on Earth.

I roam bookstores, city avenues.
Clips of the daily news
Blot out distant, unspoken
Corporate human trafficking—all in our state.
Round up cattle. You know,
The shadowy figures in slick coats—
They'll take you to a special lab
Test your I.Q. out one by one,
Pistol whip and taser your senses
To dim the lights and

Ask if
Your catastrophic missile
Wiped out
My country of sanity?

Copy down
What tears may mean.
Yeah, you held a chain
But every utterance you ever heard
Trembles beneath. Midnight
To sunlight.
Devils starving greasy kids,
Not a chance saved
In their basements.

Black eyes
Never warding off
A teacher's curious stare.
Find my sources in a book,
Share your aged beer
And never believe
I bit you like a vampire
But never left a mark.
You just can't see it.

Accept the fact
It will not be copied for you.
I never rewrite it
From my bloody fountain pen.

Lament / Ascent

Diary without a cause,
Look at how you came to be.

We curled close together
When nobody knew our wretched nights.

Poets may conceal themselves
Into bathroom stalls
Tending to ice the anxiety,
Tending to light neural fires.

Diary without a cause,
You filled my time with consolation,
An aloe remedy
Applied gently to my soul.

Diary without a cause,
Palpable prose becomes the sweetest find
Like the outlook from scaling Duquesne Incline.

My skin will one day wilt,
Unwritten memory will drift into a fog.
But this art resists the fishhook
Bait of mortality. You'll always
Have a pulse
Whenever checked.

Uncovering more—spreading truth,
I still know the world is
Fighting a war we cannot win
Loving in a land we dare not sin.

Look at what we may spawn,
Look at what we must do
Diary without a cause.

Forget-Me-Nots   ~ *For Tara*

Petite on the window sill,
The blue shimmer remained from sunlight;
This jar of forget-me-nots,
Singing to afternoon
Growth.
The bride
Who had survived
Hodgkin's lymphoma
Gave me
This centerpiece sentiment
Days after their wedding
I had not attended.

Graciously, days later, I kept an eye
On the mosaic pieces
On my nude palm.

It all became clear
From the photos she posted
After their small-town wedding
Filled with blue sky tide.
They gave color
To smitten matrimony.

I wish I witnessed
That home plate happiness
Of softly spoken vows,
The bride and groom
In early autumn
Together…
I wish I witnessed
Her healthy glow,
As our Sun finally envied Earth.

Mental Steam

Damn. Blurred by a working mind.
Remaining time jailed by
A poetry college class discussion
This Monday evening,
Spring in full bloom.
Coeds basking carelessly from window's view.
More reason to say
Damn.

It's not even necessary
To sit so long here
For our cryptic (yet quite zen) professor.
She crams desks into a boxed universe
As we spend dinner time
Tapping chopsticks on a wormy Auden,
Sighing over Page 674.
Dusty blackboards and
Carolina blue packets.
No memory of these sluggish seconds
Will bedazzle a diploma.

Softness stirs. Toes digging into socks.
It's nearly 6 o'clock. Beads of sweat belch under pits
And so does
Frothy mucus
Dripping down through my lungs.
Eyes are open but we're all
Lounging into a coma.
Come on, professor.
I pride poetry like Whitman,
Revered the strokes of his beard. Yet,
I'd rather paint this classroom's concrete
With melted Hershey bars

Than doze off to her still life that makes
Kinkade paintings roar with stock exchange bedlam.
I grope this pencil like a sex fiend;
Thumb and finger
Speeding up after a steamy caramel cappuccino.
I press onward, in thought,
Like those black birds blackmailing Wallace.

The Pub

I sip my rum with a somber face,
Flushing out this tawdry night.
The ceiling bursts out blue colors.
People are out of place.

My plush stool warms with caution.
Others are an incoming midnight tide—
Sardine-scented tongues
Toast their glasses together.

Empty pride.

Coloring Box Confessions

A young soul
Always chooses
The brightest color.

Red: Lips. Hearts. Blood.
         Blushing. Devils. On Mars.
         Wheel barrows.
         Surging eyes of those white mice.
         Ketchup meant to accompany fries.
         Bow ties. Christmas sweaters. Exit signs.
         Stop signs.

Blue: Earth's costume (with splotches of sibling Green).
         Seas vacuuming maps.
         Winter's font. Snowman's invisible shoulder.
         Sky. On a good day.
         Tears. Too visible...on a bad day.
         Royal tapestries and superhero costumes.
         Swimming pool liquid.
         Foundation for American pride.

Green: Grass scribblers, bottom of the page. We laid that
         paper down,
         Filled the branches of irregular trees. Dragons galore.
         Waxy details of the ooze.
         Earth's continents.
         Poison bottles, serum of "XX."
         Money. Bills flying from D.J. turntables.

Violet: The grudge and its exodus. A slice of fire over a
         base of ice.

Brown: Lumberjack in effect.
         Soil.
The damn dirt stain of your whitest shirt— it's crap!

Yellow: Easter eggs. Carnival lights. Acidic August suns.
         Corn. Popcorn. Unicorn's mane.
         Sand. Sandy feet.
         Pee in the snow.
         Hay near the horses.
Yield to the turning school buses.

The Ms. Fay of College

—Thank you S.G. for the inspiration to this

She wore heavy eye-shadow, dazzled by a dress.
A moxie that Sinatra would sing to—striving for high class.
High heels hiding a shorter stature, I must confess.

Auburn black hair bouncin' and flowin'
When she perked up to talk to her gals.
Italian as the Colosseum—yet soft-spoken.

When I finished some pints and played some pool,
I witnessed the backroom bar green light
Glow against her—hooked me in like that Gatsby fool.

She likely didn't even remember my face.
We took a cinema class together—
Islands apart and distant, that was the case.

After waggin' my tail—I broke the ice.
Tipsy as a Jenga set, the words
Cascaded out to roll some hoary dice:

"You look familiar," I didn't lie.
Her eyebrow curled up, asking:
"From where?" with a starry eye.

"That one book cover, called *The Great Gatsby*," I replied.
(I wasn't too sure of her literary taste)
I knew this declaration wouldn't kill my pride.

She gaped and her hazel eyes widened:
"I love that book!"

Guitar Labor

~Dedicated to Steel City Coffeehouse (Phoenixville, Pa.)

Those 7 p.m. sets.
Mic test.

1...2...

The ceiling's cobalt gown swallowed notes
Above a grizzled guitar player,
Practicing intervals for his pen name's label.

He continues to carry cadences...

By day, the host sulks in a cubicle.
By night, he is the town's David Gilmour
For a coffeehouse's misfit clan.

This host never acknowledged spiritual encounters;
His closest instance was said to be a Pearl Jam concert.
The circles of shadows filed in and out,
Outnumbering the host's half-steps.

He cradles his body
Taming the unruly Gibson.

I'm stirred in a silent booth not knowing
The lights have dimmed.
Electric haze.

I make side notes of sidetracked people:
Shape-shifting queens with deceptive gazes
And no concerns for speed. They are selling sins
To a smack-talking street cat
While wearing earrings in the shape of New Jersey.

The climb to fame
In café club dismay
Pits our struggling world
In one night's rush. A rally of mullet barons
And college dropouts
Yelling, "BEST NIGHT EVER!"
Each and every hour.

The host thanked Nashville muses
From country road commitments.
He succeeded in tonight's after-hours rhythm.

A reverence for his constant composition,
Snoozing and cruising
Across unkempt bars.
His most soulful decade earned
Scarlet finger scars.

Upward

Pining to believe
I died somewhere calm.
The sway of Appalachian forests
Earth's endless breeze.

You see it in aeromancy—
The clouds shift towards an opening
For my soul's next escape.
Let this sheer light
Glow galaxy far

So that my last celestial breath
Will whisper over shaded vines.
A steady rise
To fading stars.

Nightmare

That yellow-spotted demon,
Rattle snake patience
Fond of its selfishness
Drank my praying blood,
Spit out a stone,
Nourished itself under blazing sun
This scaly, Mexican menace...
Evening eluder
With an unexpected appetite.

I faced it with my firm stare—
Couldn't dodge its dance
Couldn't evade the entropy
Couldn't kill a cavern king...

Everything then faded to white.

Eternal Summers

We explored the hilly hay fields in a barefoot run
Sweaty from backyard baseball and a creekside croon.

We foolishly spit our laughter into neon sun
As it coasted between clouds that 21st of June.

We gathered at the embankment of sycamore trees
Hours after getting stung by those damn bees

To passionately discuss and protect
An old mason jar that we had kept
In lieu of attracting fireflies at sunset.

The mystic glowing cooled us down—
A hush of the innocence found
Us revealing a depth within, an unlit pyre
We had never known the summer prior.

We awed at the serene, illuminated glory.
Hardly a sound but waning cricket choir.

We knew *this* moment would be a story
To tell our kids by a blazing campfire.

Status Update

An accentuated opinion
Mental hiccups from the bohemian mind
Oh—the humor my friends will come to find!

A cathartic touch and a scathing dose
Of ethos mixed with paltry pathos

Because... we're all simpleton poets.

What I Should Have Said

Maybe silly thoughts
Of a time machine
Won't change our past one bit.

Maybe inhaling every painful detail
Of the present is not
Particularly kind.

The hardships, the sacrifices made in vain—inkblots
From before.

You and I—we tore out pages.
Tore out love,
Tore out hope.

Yet, we befriended a silent courage
Painted certainly to teach—instilled patience
To grieve greater worldly affairs.

Words are my maze,
But I wish to aim an arrow
On absolute amends—
Clearing out conscious dust
And torn up letters off the floor
So I may not walk alone
Out the door.

I may not fit the high bill, in your eyes,
To be brought home to the parents
And admired—
But a chance,
Just *a chance*
Would have made all the difference.

Copper Sun Corrupted

White light angels
All alone

Whispering for serenity.
I hear too many voices in despair.

Sunflower fields withered
From a copper sun corrupted—
Obscene flames with no care.

No American lung
Spanning the sands of west Texas
Will survive this caustic highway zone.

Someday I'll see you through a song,
When the evening news isn't so somber—
Days far beyond the summer
Alienated by an endless drone.

Super Powers

We handcrafted our capes
From beach towels or drapes.
We color-coded our souls
From comic book dynamite.
We were just kids—
Tyler, Gavin, Schmidty, Jay, and me.
Anything was possible.

    Now it's 20 years later. Schmidty died.
    Our beloved corner store closed down.
    Busy dust has settled
    In my kitchen cabinets.
    The alley cat eats more food
    Than I do.

More than ever, I dare ask
The rest of the mighty dream makers:
Do you conquer workday depression?

Tyler's invisibility is now seclusion
    From a prior conviction.
Jay's only flight
    From a routine corporate conference
    Goes red eye
    From Vancouver back to misty Newark.

Gavin once breathed fire
    But now he's trying to suppress
    Cigarette habits
    And the concepts of cancer.
We wanted to read girls' minds.
    Now I read legal divorce papers.
    Her piercing blade of kryptonite.

There is no muscle, no agile way
To deflect the downpours.
Our estranged veins start to age
Faster than a comic book's
Wilted and forgotten back page.

At times, I'm not so sure
There's enough strength
To be human
Because every human falls.

Ms. Farm Town Millennial

~Based on an encounter I had in Kutztown with a unique person

I want to live in a Victorian style home
One day— when my paychecks are bigger
Than the family thrift store salary
Holding me down.

I'm done with this farm town.
The university is full of idiots.
2.0 GPA to get in? No wonder.

I'm German, but I really don't feel like it.
I don't drink beer
I don't scarf down burgers
Like those frat boys that passed along here—
They'll pass out in the park later.
My family is strict with their German genes.
And thank God
We've all stayed skinny.

You see those shirts?
Hanging on that rack—baggy is in.
They make any girl look pregnant.
I'd die in those outfits.

I'm in love with Ireland.
My friend from the Poconos may gift me
An airline ticket to go with him.
You know what I'll do first? Drive to Drumcliffe.
Drop daisies on Yeats's grave.
I'm serious when I say it—Ireland is my Disney Land.

I hate people.
I love *Beauty and the Beast*. I know every word from the movie.
But I despise *The Little Mermaid*.
I can't stand her smug voice.
Can't stand that tomato slush hair.
Halloween is coming up soon.
Don't trust college girls that dress like Ariel.

I might go as someone from an Iroquois-Indian tribe.
I just bought these feathers and teal jewels.
My playlist in the store is set for the classics.
I just drift away in the music.

Her Name Was Colour

Her name was Colour
Raised from a clan so gray
Little did she witness
The world behind window shades.

Finest hours faded
Before any moment of joy
Her name was Colour
Never kissed a single boy.

Amid the daily customer drivel,
Colour carefully recited written lines.
Just a teacup income
Taming phone calls from sordid lives.

Colour coined her own favorite phrase,
"Embrace all these remaining days!"
In her private pocket journal.
An attuned deep-sea diver of knowledge,
She felt the gravitas of Broadway plays.

Colour wrote complex poems
On how *The Fox and The Hound*
Consequently geared her to lose trust
In family and friends after being abandoned.

Colour walked among crowded corridors—
Saddened by life's myths and metaphors.
Clever and weird—she was keenly sharpened
By the hope that love was a growing garland.

Graduating
~Written in May of 2012

Sometimes you must let go of something so dear.
Sometimes you must face your greatest fear.
Directions and clouds never looked so unclear.
It was known, it was said at college
While we thrived:
The world will spin seasons into a year.
Then two. Then three. Then four.

Doors open and close.
Vehicles were meant to steer.
It's the time to define where you were, how you came here.
Share a laugh or shed a tear.
These memories are based on what we miss
What's been created by a friend, foe, or peer.
These memories are heavier than the luggage we brought.

So...

Embrace the caffeinated all-nighters,
The lessons taught or blunders we mistook.
Break down that blithe undergrad life
As you'll go places, according to a famous book.

From our decisions of heart, to the sights we see
Is it safe to say we are finally free?

Time to obtain that degree.

Part Two

Tikkun Olam

"To heal the Earth"—how can it be?
Perhaps first
We must
Have our minds clearly see.

Live and prosper.
Find your world worth breathing for.
Sink into the snow, grieve with relentless rain,
But always try to capture
The warmest sun rays that are hidden.
Yes they may be like dreams,
They may be imaginary seeds.
Grow with them!

Especially when nobody bothers bringing you light.

Big Lollipop, Small Child

An oversized baton
The marching pretender.
Adoring comforts of candy,
Mouthful of sweet, sweet
Syrup. Stretching
That gabbing jaw
And suppressing the gums—no guilt,
Thrusting a tongue.

This bovine mind…
Sweet, silly child!

Cyclist

~*Dedicated to John R. Anczarski, who founded The Pink Pedal charity (8/16/1990 – 6/22/2010)*

This generous son of rural Ringtown
Dared to gladly stand out.
He never wasted time, nor settled down.
This clever Eagle Scout

Remained loyal and always held his word.
Pursuing pilot goals, he never broke laws
But was bound to fly above any bird.

He never held an ounce of hate,
Ultimately leading towards a noble cause
Few would ever try to imitate:

Cycling cross-country in the summer. A way
To increase breast cancer awareness—
The Pink Pedal had started with little delay.

An unyielding and sweltering day by day
Journey of 4 cyclists starting in good ole Pa.
Pursuing sands of a California bay.
This excursion shed light on a purposeful getaway:

An Illinois radio interview, camping out off the street
Riding the paceline through Route 66 heat
Befriending a breast cancer survivor that lent a hand,
Meeting the Albuquerque mayor and a mariachi band.

It all came to a halt at the 29th day—John had been taken away
By a reckless car driver, striking him head-on.
The agony of loss—the brightness had suddenly gone.
A numb severance for those wanting to hold on.
Loved ones sported shirts designed with Anczarski Strong.

John became an influencer before smart phone influencers
took modern stage.
A catalyst among others, he shared wisdom and a natural spark.
He lived as a nomad filled with desire—a selfless spirit that
can never age.

August 17, 2012

A dreadful summer drought
Since turning the plump college tassel.
No feasible, grand career
Launching from today.

I mask pain of shrill setbacks
Smoother than eraser tip enamel.

I pray for a new path,
Sending my name
To the human resources game,
Waiting like a bed-bound patient
Injected by a daily IV of shame.

I'm not old enough for six-figures
Nor am I experienced enough
For double digits per hour.

I've walked out the door
To drink every cloned crystal
Of some carbonated concoction—
No bloody fountain of youth.

Like other college grads know,
The dreaded four letter word
D   E   B   T
Hangs over the head
Any direction we go.

I'll visit my college again,
The place once called home.
The void of nobody familiar
Alters it to some colorful graveyard—
Memories remain.

I don't belong in these parts anymore.
Can't further my credentials into
Another pile of certified papers
Casted for a painful conclusion.

I don't belong in some airbrushed philosophy
Where utter nakedness
Of flawed American minds
Coerce the system
To weasel their way up front
While upstanding morals
Are pushed aside
By the mural of mortals
Fastened by black ties.

I don't belong on a false mountain.
Rich stealing from poor.
Younger people scorned
For speaking out against the snake's sin.

My mother's forests are pillaged,
Picked apart for some sterling
Huxley enterprise. Water will continue
To give an aftertaste of oil.

I walk away from the college town,
Avoid the hazards of my hometown.
I find myself best in a lush forest.
Free from the critical noise.

I locked eyes with a lone falcon
Perched on a high-rise tower.
He observed the miles I drifted away to spend.
The falcon pitied my loss of willpower
Not knowing where my trouble would end.

Trying To Get By
~*Written in October of 2012*

The vampire. Accustomed
To his cupboard of canned olives
Calmly dials for a 3 a.m. dinner guest
Curling moist hairs
Under his thick brow.
His sleek studio apartment
Towers over the city.
Sounds of endless traffic whirrs below
While pet bats are screeching
From the sounds
Of his stereo's blithe saxophone jazz.

Drought. *Drought.*
Cold pale sweat only remains
Beading along the bridge of his nose.
He winces at how the "marinara" stains
Won't fade from a few kitchen tiles—
A sly alibi for new acquaintances.

Goodness knows
He is still in recovery.
Struggling to be normal
Step by step.
This brooding immortal
Cannot openly share
Old disasters.

Claudia's Coffee Guests

Sonny

A friend who believes in the supernatural.
He collects dreamcatchers, would debate
All the vegan qualms— his neo-hippie guise
Saves some money, but secludes himself
At home
Long enough to try to bathe
His mother's Daschund hound (the poor thing).
He then said on his own, at the new condo
Bed bugs were somehow plotting his demise.

Robert

The last time I saw him,
He couldn't figure out
What his life's "niche" would be.

We dated
As 8th grade klutzes.
We met
Working on a shop class birdhouse.

He was the charitable one,
For 5 years
Supplying kisses
After early morning drives—
Dropping me off at the store
For work I always despised.

Routinely lent me his cotton hoody.
Winter's best warmth tucked in—
Fresh out of the dryer.
I have yet to return it to him.
I wonder, as the café's glass door clangs:
Has he found his niche?

Yolanda

I turn at the table and see Yolanda, yapping away.
She nursed my Robert wounds up at college.
She advised—more like forced—me
To delete his phone number.
I refused, and refused, and still refused
To accept the painful reality of getting dumped.
An ugly chunk of Autumn weeks wasted.

Yolanda had trouble
Juggling majors, juggling
Appalling adultery—
So, she transferred
To a prestigious school
Still carrying her trigger-happy mouth
With a side of trigger-happy flirtation—
I hope her cohorts found out!

Evelyn

She lived through college like a bullseye
Was on her back.
Took self-defense classes,
Sneered at the barstool hacks
Trying to hit on her.
I'd give her a 7,
But the frat clan felt she was a 9.
She felt vindicated to her motive,
Always stepped on toes
To get ahead.
Her sister was murdered.

But, her memory survived
All too well.
I'd feel a bloody strife
If innocence, justice, and mourning
A loved sibling stood in our way
To just live a damn life.

***

The café door made its final clang.

Risk & Logic

~*Written in March of 2013.*
Dedicated to the poet Daniel Abdal-Hayy Moore

Risk was born with a shark tooth-shaped toenail.
Logic was a finely combed newborn.

Risk boogie-boarded down the steps.
Logic wore a helmet.

Risk crawled into the sewers.
Logic played Monday morning soccer.

Risk pulled the girl's hair.
Logic sipped sugar-free lemonade.

Risk stared too close to television.
Logic read the Bible.

Risk packed beef jerky.
Logic came to lunch with carrot sticks.

Risk ran into walls.
Logic paced himself.

Risk cheated off tests.
Logic studied to bedtime.

Risk reveled in being a meddler.
Logic sincerely asked questions.

Risk watched MTV.
Logic watched History Channel.

Risk rarely showered.
Logic squirted hand sanitizer.

Risk called everybody by their stereotype.
Logic learned through honest discussion.

Risk cursed in emotion.
Logic bit the tongue.

Risk blasted his earphones.
Logic accompanied a soft run of Mozart.

Risk wouldn't buy birthday cards.
Logic cleanly sealed everything in envelopes.

Risk retired for bed at 3:30 a.m.
Logic slept soundly the full 8 hours.

Risk didn't apply for part-time jobs.
Logic earned and accumulated.

Risk bought all the bells and whistles.
Logic rewarded himself on holidays.

Risk smoked a carton of cigarettes.
Logic filtered all his thoughts.

Risk peeked at cleavage.
Logic said 'please' and 'thank you'.

Risk let his unruly hair grow.
Logic kept his retainer.

Risk shook all the birds' nests.
Logic attended Sunday church.

Risk never wore a condom.
Logic abstained until marriage.

Risk kept too many guns lying around the house.
Logic learned the first time around.

Feign Civil Glory

Sometime near a winter-worn malady
This all occurred to me:

A bus ride conversation
Orchestrated by a baby boomer,
Unwavering male passenger—
JFK was his heyday.

My cold, cough, and temper
Mixed with his Sunday sermon
Clawed at my erratic mind.

His utterances did not matter
As I could not hear his words.
No acoustics except muffled rambling.

My eyes tempt for a removal
Of this awkward snowy crusade.
I calculate deceptive nods
While we approach a tunnel.
All for his poor, neighborly heart.

Cursed

~Written in October of 2013

My mind has been lathered
Like a cold stone in a hot soup—
An inorganic mix of madness
Boiling for the witch's brew.

Black smoke— blocking my course
Spawns a driving force.
Shrill, unwanted ravens
Plucking and prying
What's left of my shelter's glue.

Aspiration and desperation
Reflect the wounded herons
Flying against changing tides.

Amid the mess—
What can I redeem?
Everything becomes a blur
Like a bad dream.

Lasting aches to my brittle spine,
I gaze through the window
Angled against fading time.
If only this glass would pop
To the pain of my scream.

Life Isn't Fair

~Written in January of 2014

A wicked lady scolded me,
"Life Isn't Fair!"
No reasoning. No humane willingness
To even have a dialogue.
She was not in the right mindset
To stab me with her adage
That was well off the point
Of my merciful plea,
What a fool she may be.

What is life, actually?
You can't package life
Only into one box—
Or stick it into one single frame,
There's multiple keys for locks,
A vast compartment that changes
Much like life does in its phases.
Life isn't just a single unsavory dish
That you throw away once, never to eat.

Life has loads of dissatisfactions;
Willfully ignorant members
Of the seven deadly sins.
There are cruel designs of fate
Meant to further and dictate
Prejudice, destitution, famine, trafficking.
The erratic roll of destiny's dice
Can plague the best person once or twice!
Death, illness, furloughs, catastrophe…

We must sacrifice wills, sacrifice pride
When choices are limited deep down inside.
We're given paths to cross
Whether by fear or by chance.

It's hard to deny—that yes,
Life will not always be fair, wicked one.
But your fragmented idea of fairness
Stains grace as your sanity is all but done.

Life is fair and life is not fair.
Both can be true. But here is the truth.
Life is a continuum.

Online Dating

Snap
      A feature photo
Reveal
      Inner-most desires
Demand
      The best attention
Pray
      For no stalkers
Question
      What this person wants
Refrain
      From numb interrogation
Schedule
      Times to talk or meet
Require
      An honest person
Move
      Along with life

West Philadelphia Visit

An aging woman in tight leggings is berated
From the roasting of summer's high noon.

She trudges an obnoxious 2-year-old in a stroller
By an abandoned aquarium shop
At 41st and Chestnut.

Nothing short of a bumpy ride.
She coughs, faintly unsure if the cigarette addiction
From her 30's is absolutely over.

Dogs bark catastrophically
In the background of broken fences.
Smacking her gums, she pulls extra weight
To the left side of her truncated body.
Long ago, her former lover assaulted her
With an aluminum bat he bought at Wal-Mart.

The sulphur scent of marijuana bathes the air.
Pigeons come, pigeons depart.
Grills sizzling a share of beef patties for all—
A sickly aroma spreads.

The woman pines for some food
But knows it's another 3 blocks to her residence.
That aquarium shop decays within helplessly
Behind the dust of jet black windows.

It's like Madoff took corruption
To a lower level of the business world—
Barren signs and cardboard cut outs
Of what life used to be, depressingly
Hanging around this sweltering day.
No materialized coverage of a police officer in sight.

A scrappy homeless man is sprawled
On a stoop platform
Vegetating slowly
While a "MONEY 4 FOOD" sign balances on his lap.

Inside Story of Goodbye

'd' and 'b' leaned on each other.
Inseparable, loyal friends
Their lines drawn parallel
Faces set on different ends.

Roommates forced to fit
In a fleeting world
Triggered borderline friction
Between these two
Constant consonants.

'd' managed the entire apartment—
Cleanliness became his forte.
 'b' buoyed foreign sailors off a shore
(For safe keeping) day by day.

'd' always meant well.
'b' meant clocking out.
'd' played the strings.
'b' buried fingers into organ keys.

'd' opened the book.
'b' shut the book.
'd' earned honors for the best.
'b' earned steady salute.
'd' held a dramatic pause.
'b' distanced himself from the rest.

First Trip To The Movies

1994 was the year.
The boy sat in a plush seat
Under an arena of dimmed lights
Inhaling a buttery, sweet aroma
For a wide, silver screen display
Located near the Coventry Mall.

Simba had sprawled
All his sorrow
Onto his lifeless father.

The whole audience couldn't fight
A tearful deluge for this lonely cub.

The young boy confronted cold insight
That death had no tomorrow.

Ever since then,
Movies ascended to
The boy's eye—

A birth within the coated filmstrip

Absorbing abstract and concrete,
Regarding visual drama so discrete

That a limbic infusion blends
Between vivid ideals, love, and sinking hardship.

October 25, 2014

A midnight chill
Near a desolate end of Doylestown
Limited my movements.
These 20-something hosts
Welcomed argyle sweaters, colored costumes,
And smoking of all sorts.

They uncorked the champagne—
Raising hell and pissing in puddles.

I eavesdropped on a time
They blabbed about
Sprinting stark naked
At 3:30 a.m.
On the New Hope-Lambertville bridge
Drunkenly praising bankruptcy.

They dug out details
From foolish photos taken:
Smashing porcelain pumpkins
In their neighbor's cornfield.

They laughed dizzyingly,
Raging uproariously
To Guns N' Roses lyrics—
The endless campfire bash
Became the bane of silence.

Part Three

Discovering Sea Glass

Cutting up life's apple and taking the core
Revealed the remains of my mind's lore.
I never knew as a wee-little newborn
What destiny's plan had in store.

The trouble is
I don't know where
The trouble began.

Perhaps years after
I tossed aside the fruit of Earth—poetry—
Into an oceanic descent of meaning, healing, taste
Deep into a salty abyss, suspended
To rot under layers of obsolete verses—a waste.

Lying on the darkest ocean floor,
Closure is hidden in a glass capsule.
Years pass—there's a pull of every grain
For answers to all of life's toil…it grew
As an object propelling against the cascade
Towards an open surface—met by shades of blue.

Incessant fog shrouded along soulless water.
This object—like my mind's eye—
Sees a distant siren's face.
Yet, I surrender my will
Drifting towards a different seaway space.

Many buoys of men, women—
Weathered treasures and sober faces
Pass by—what remains a special souvenir?
I sense the rip currents to elude.
Innocence broken from what a storm chases.

Crashing back on a beach, finally land
Earning the spray of sunlight, clumps of sand
Showcased as a new form, though not perfect,
This migrating life is strong enough to connect

Generations absorbed
Into mighty tall tales,
Musing deep ideas and smooth observations
Crafted into pure chaos, every atom is regaled!

Prom Queen at Heart
-Dedicated to C.A.M.

Her husky, pastel neck
Held a set of pearls
Set against a scarlet dress.
Glasses routinely slipping
Down her nose.
Blushing, she clenched
The quarterback's hand
Of a young man
That kept a promise
Dating back
To a 7th grade class trip.

How could he ever turn around
On the deal they made?
She lent him most of her lunch.
This former new boy had struggled
Adapting to a new school, also bound
By an alcoholic single mother.

Now he's laced within the
Velvet rope of social ranks:
Lacrosse. Debate. Jazz band.
He could care less (tonight)…

She spotted him rides afterward
When his mom couldn't lend a hand.

April mist, sweeping winds—what scene
Was this girl's favorite?
Perfect pictures on a rustic porch.
An iridescent crown topped it all.
His limo stationed itself
Against a leafy backdrop bloom.

She had wept for years
Devoid of any true friends—
Was it her fascination
From offbeat, mystic books?
Was her heavier frame
The cause to cruel cat-calls?
Were her thick sneezes—
Popular upon teases—
The straw that broke
The social camel's back?
Even teachers would glare
At her flowing hair.

For tonight, this imperfect girl
Became close to perfect.
At least good enough.
She rested her head, on his shoulder
And he didn't mind.
This law school hopeful
Did her justice
Swelling up with pride
Not just for himself—
But for her.

May 24, 1941

~Dedicated to Bob Dylan (Robert Allen Zimmerman)

You are a rare comet ripping through the sky
One we'll never see again, I do not lie.
Your words became waves upon this planet
A mystic artisan that culture can't forget.

An unknown among hearts, history, and smoking sages
Crafted the world—rugged and raw— deep in pages
For endless generations to listen on play
Baring the joys and pains too hard to convey.

What resided in the poet's mind
Beyond his Shakespearean scope?
Uncommon multitudes will always remain.
I can't help but struggle to cope

How to forage through this new world
When one sad day
The burning flame
Will cease to bring light untamed.

Strange Photographer

Capturing…
What a cliché!
As if I cared for the split second
When the zoom finely displayed
An out-of-touch mother
And a disheveled daughter.

They contemplated questions
From the divorce.
They sat in my local diner,
Sifting plastic menus.

I must have heard (and thought) too much
Before I pushed the button.

The mother, a moody Reaganite
Kept cobweb-filled closets
Packed with sagging memories.
Sensitive cuts and
A willingness quite wrinkled.
Something below middle-class.
Religion abandoned her stratosphere.
Whiskey remained a casual scent.

The daughter—labeled an 'accident'
Wore raggedy hair
Sang Elvis songs.
She never knew by this eleventh year of years
Braces would sever ties to her school peers.

The daughter eyed me brightly
For my fatherly features.
(Stubble, a fine black coat, white apron)
They ordered the western omelet with juice—
A natural purchase.

They needed to bond this morning.

The mother sent a dirty look
Forcing me to fumble the camera
Much like her decision-making.
"Give a good shot," she chided.

"Surely," I sighed.
Only those espresso Mondays
Would I discover
A daughter's pink sweater, sleeves torn
And a mother's loaded cigarette mouth
To be disturbingly beautiful.

This picture should live on
For the limited years
They have left together.
A beacon of love's misunderstandings.

Mistakes
~*Written in February of 2015*

I'm near the crisp age
Of living a quarter-century life
And admitting my mistakes.
I'm an Irish guilt trip—damned and doomed
To feel as though
Nothing is perfect
And that I cannot go wrong.

Maybe that's why
Scorpions sting my cerebellum
At the sight of
Cop cars driving by.

Officers will point out
Our driving follies
(Whether intentional or not)
And we pay the price
From igniting red and blue lights—
It leaves a flustered feeling.

Nobody's rewarded for petty accomplishments...
Holding the door,
Not letting the laundry sit.
Matchmaking for a friend.

That's how I've come to grasp in life—
Walking, sitting, standing, running, or driving.
Mistakes will come and go, but desire
To earn approval or sell a thought
Is what makes accomplishments
A sort of salvation from our dread.

Adversity

~Dedicated to Kobe Bryant

Belief in yourself comes in many ways.

Through others' eyes is one.
Through your best friends is another.

Maybe it generates from trusted advisors.

Then, the toughest critic
Could be dropped into your world
To make things extremely difficult.

You set your sights and goals
So sky high
That their scorning clouds
Made you wish
You never tried.

I want to wish
The best
To those that hold a heavy, wounded heart.
The bravest people
We all may know fight the internal warfare
Of disposing hope and turning
Rotten, wrongful actions
Into better experiences.

One day, you'll be ready
to escape their downpours and prevail
in a streaking sunlight.
Before you know it,
You're facing the mirror,
Telling yourself
It got better.

Park Bench Plaque

Pulling tight my scarf
On this blustery winter day
I walk downtown and return
To the park. I seek out a bench

Shaded by oak trees. This bench
Is a dedicated structure to him.
My wife and I were his only neighbors—
Nobody else claimed this.

His legacy remains pressed
On a silver plate—a simple saying
From Calvin and Hobbes.
Future walkers will glance at
His life's last known remnant.

***

Now I sit beside you—
Another penny spent
Another year gone by
Another leaf fallen.
An unintentional tear
Streams down my cheek
On the anniversary that you passed.

Kids can run by, crawl over
Your recycled reincarnation

But they will never know the depths
Of your selfless support—
Finding my wallet, shoveling snow,
Catering church picnics
And midnight bedside manner
For when my wife suffered through hospice.
Now I must pack away all remaining relics.

***

I choose to sip hot cocoa,
Whisper about my affairs
Since everything changed
Without her here.

And your affairs…aside from pigeon shit?
No matter. The quiet ones always tolerate
Life's little messes.

I feel a spry cardinal
Is all the peace you'll need.

Good company and observance
Nestled over diminished leaves.

The World

~Written in November of 2015

Why is it
That nations, races, and religions
Are always fighting?
Hate—spreading like a virus.

Stealing money
Exhausting energy
Threatening chaos
Just to seize control.

Opening this can of worms
Upon the world
And debating every micro debacle
Passes on
Prideful, petulant, and pretentious
Seeds of thought
To grow
In everlasting anatomy
Of every human.

One day
Will we drop these weapons?
Will there be reconciliation over revenge?
Will legions of blind
Cease fire
On their doctrine of outdated beliefs
Into someone's chest
Without realizing
Every life is equal?
With all majesty stripped from death
Is every tomb equal?
Persistent prayers—

But no way preserve a reasonable future
Unless we exercise tolerance
To a greater degree.

Thousands of years in civilization
And billions of people
Can step forward united
Or surge mobs into oblivion.

Wake Up
~Written in March of 2016

1. To Being Up

Dark, muted rumblings
Breathe with vague visions…
The bumble bee drone
Swarming,
Swelling to a burst:
BUZZ BUZZ BUZZ

Soft opening to brightness,
Musty scents. Slap the snooze.
Cold air with just underwear
In the comfort of a comforter.
Toes dancing in defiance.
Mucus squirming to back of throat—
Muscles moving, tongue welcoming teeth
And the dreaded conscious afloat
To this newfound day, a medley of cerebral souvenirs:
Hardships
Errands
  Dues
  Emotions
  Expectations
Stress not yet conquered…
The past life's mishaps.

2. To The Shower Head

Oh! (Underwear tossed)
Consuming light—
A laboratory white space
Readying this nude creature
For unwilling renewal.
To rinse and shed the dead
Skin cells.
Turning the knob, gently.
Step down. Just go all at once—
Need to get to work!

SSSS...

Militia of liquid needles
Splashing, covering
Raiding arctic chill,
Dialing it to boiling hot!
Dumbly, biting the lip
Skin welcomes heat.
Slippery soap,
Dabbling moisture,
Rising temperature
Calming a set of closed eyes.

3. To Breaking Out of Home

Morning news static:
"46 degrees today, partly cloudy..."
While slicing a bagel,
Peeling an aged orange.

Adding on Nutella may sweeten the deal.
Brewing a hot cup of coffee.
Begin the caffeine rush.
Prep the hair, pull out some socks.
Organize some mail envelopes from the bank.
Finger guess a track jacket,
Snag the briefcase—pee, flush
Bolt out the door.

4. To The Commute

The morning radio
Serves as a conversation starter
(Kobe's final game is coming...
...Villanova can cement Wright's legacy)
While the car grumbles against its gears—
It drives along patterned roads
You're conditioned to seeing routinely.

School buses slow down.
Blinkers all red—set to stop.
Weeping mothers say goodbye
To their jaded, eye-rolling 2nd graders.

"It's only one day."

Ireland & Northern Ireland

~Written in September of 2017

Ireland and Northern Ireland
Has owned up to its history of perdition—
Nothing scared us away of its past condition.

We embarked on the ultimate dreamscape
Of what modern trailblazers shaped upon
Seeking out any possible landscape
To map out endeavors starting each dawn.

Cliffs of Moher—an eye candy
To all of nature's majesty.

Galway—a festival of shop street colors
Surrounded by harbors, the long walk
Enriched by dingle-gin ice cream flavors.

Yeats's grave hidden among a misty woodland
Neighboring the curvy awe of Benbulbin highland.

A stone wall surrounds the epicenter of Derry
At first glance, it seems dreadful and scary—
But the city is rising to bridge manageable peace.

Giant's Causeway—a fabled shoreline treat
Soaked hexagon stones under your feet.

Belfast, the city was a crowning jewel
For size and pace, any tourist will rule
It to be a delightful desire with takeaways:
Queen's University, gardens, markets, waterways—
The Titanic museum, a tour with somber and splendor
Street corners of fine graffiti, a city hall to render
A fruitful and growing history—
Belfast has a share of documented highs and lows,
But we saw beauty on a mountain called Napoleon's Nose.

Underdogs

~Dedicated to my Pap: 02/26/1943 – 08/20/2018

A soft, but firm discourse
United a region's residents
From Septa stations or any Wawa run:

"Go Birds!"

As 2017 carried into 2018
A superstitious flow
Blended by fear, driven by hope
Suspended itself
Into the hearts and minds
Of Philadelphia Eagles fans.

The frozen January track
Gave an unanticipated pathway:
Relying on an old friend at quarterback.
Nick Foles once thrilled Philly
With head coach Chip Kelly.

It was a wild, short stint—but like a crazy karma thief
Foles declined as a Ram, Andy Reid released him as a Chief...

Only for Foles to reunite with the midnight green
As a backup to Carson Wentz.
Nobody would've foreseen
The duty to work with Plan B.
Carson came out of the medical tents
After Wentz tore his ACL by week 14.

The hauntings of old failures came crashing down:
Fog Bowl, Bryce Paup, the death of Jerome Brown
Fitzgerald's TD hat trick, Ronde Barber's pick-six
All tackling the task ahead; no Peters, Sproles, or Hicks.

The media and sports betting never gave the #1 seed a shot
When Atlanta came to town, animosity grew a lot
Towards the talking-head experts waving Philly's white flag
For a Divisional Round game where scoring was a drag.

Torrey Smith caught the key ball, bounced off Keanu Neal,
Just getting 3 extra points at the half felt like a steal.
Foles shook off the rust to deliver a sharp second half
While Blount and Ajayi rumbled past Falcon staff.
The edge-of-your-seat suspense came to a breathless close,
A 4th down in the red zone just missed Julio Jones.

Minnesota Vikings were fresh off a miracle thriller
Their first drive of the NFC title felt like a buzz killer:
Déjà vu all over again? Just short of another Super Bowl berth?
A Patrick Robinson pick-six changed it all, for what it's worth.
Eagles' offense hit on all cylinders versus the Purple People
Eaters,
Foles launching it to his weapons—for once we were world
beaters!

For the Super Bowl, this was it. One more test upstream,
U.S. Bank Stadium in Minneapolis didn't feature a Viking team
As the Eagles were one step closer from the ultimate dream.
The New England Patriots entered the field to "Crazy Train"
Pursuing a repeat of 13 years ago, which caused Philly pain.

Both teams first exchanged field goals for a 3-3 tie.
With quarter 1 waning, Nick Foles then let it fly—
34 yards to Alshon Jeffery, snagging it up on the jump.

9-3

The next big score was LeGarrete Blount's 21-yard thump.

15-3

New England returned the favor with two scores of their own,
Yet a missed trick play to Tom Brady dropped like a stone.

15-12

A dump pass and dash of Corey Clement set up a goal line stand
As the first half clock waned, stress stirred with any Philly fan.
The highlight to end all highlights in Philly sports history
A 4th and goal huddle was a thing of mystery:
Will a running back get a carry? Will Foles pass it?
None of the above.
Snap to Clement, pitch to Trey Burton, he sets up a pass
Foles wide open at the end zone corner.
Millions just fell in love.

22-12

The Halftime festivities came and went.
Then Rob Gronkowski shredded Eagle defense.

22-19

Clement caught another big pass, a miracle ball from Foles.

29-19

Patriots receiver Chris Hogan burned through Philly's defensive holes.
29-26

The Eagles tacked on another field goal to extend the lead.

32-26

Yet Gronkowski struck again; Eagles' hopes started to bleed.

32-33

The adversity was not daunting enough to fret St. Nick.
His decisions—even a key 4th down throw—would click
The final touchdown was a well angled Zach Ertz dart,
He launched headfirst passed the goal line with heart.

38-33

Tom Brady was given 2 minutes
To (once again) make a comeback
Until a blazing Brandon Graham came on the attack
To make a historic strip-sack.

Fortune reversed possessions, Eagles gained full force
To put the game away, Lombardi Trophy on course.
Merely adding a field goal by Jake Elliott's boot—
Just 65 seconds away from putting haters on mute.

41-33

One last drive, time was ticking away,
The Patriots' chances were looking gray.
9 seconds left on the clock. A 52-yard pathway.
Brady dodged a sack, in the pocket he would stay.

He gave it one monumental heave!
Hands hit the ball, it dropped—bouncing on the turf!
Eagles fans—shocked at awe—celebrated around Earth!
The 58-year title drought finally came to a close
Green confetti fell like snow, a perfect dose
For the faithful who deserved it the most!

The Philadelphia Eagles were Super Bowl Champions.

Liberty

A Cambodian sea turtle
Spends 95 percent of its life
On the ocean floor waiting
For its prey.

I have spent late evenings
Feeling like this turtle—
Tactical, starving.
Yet, alone and suppressed
By cruel demands
Society has brought upon
Life, liberty, and the pursuit of happiness
Of a modern college graduate.

Experience is devised, somehow
Through the rigor of books, papers,
Projects, and penniless nights. I feel
The waves crashing in
Once I'm let loose.

We have to swim
Viciously
Within our strengths. Maybe even
Cheat, lie, manipulate
Just like Leo Callahan
Digging out of Eastern State.

Tacking on eccentric experiences
In a new age
Where companies refuse
Full-time benefits,
Outsourcing to eccentric lands.

It's all out of my hands—
Submit credentials to wait and see.
Beyond that task, I must
Modify the disintegrated
Outlook of liberty.

Ricci (Homage to *Bicycle Thieves*)

Oh Bruno, sweet Bruno!
May your shrewd mother shame me!
She'll hold in the dagger
That will never set my heart free.

Bruno, blessed Bruno!
A meager income,
And any means of an evening dish
Were my intentions—follies of a fallen man.

Are we all bicycle thieves?
To paint signboards
That we have no heart for—
We must make the country, the forefathers,
And the children proud.
Crushed dreams—
Our daily grievance!

Do we all dwell
In a Denaro sea?

Rise

~Written shortly after August 28, 2019
(The day I passed my NBCOT Exam)

I must rise to pass the test
I must rise to win this grueling game
Waiting to be certified alongside
Golden names of the best

That have trailblazed long before.
Unattainable, displeased up to now,
I seek the acceptance much more
Pushing myself to what I can allow.

I must hold my bulletproof head
A little higher as the days go.
I smile, glisten, and wipe off dread
At the thought of some halo

Crowning itself for all the world to see.
No human saw the 7 years of dank sweat
Or time it took to keep myself clean.
Will I make it? Can I fake it? Must I fret?

Down I started, a dark and dusty mine
Searching: Figures, facts, a way to go
Up. All underlying reasons why
Fate shined a light to me, bestowed.

My history harbors on the wait of expedition.
I clench with fear and prepare to climb
Out from the mine, it is my sole mission

To breathe air of the sweetest volition
To rise from the concrete and unholy trap
To start the course of highest ambition
To plot my ways on Tabula Rasa's map.

Millennials

-Written in December of 2019

Make way for a new generation.
An uncommon collection of outcasts,
A fury of sharp intellects
A crew of creative dynamics—
Some craving only Netflix,
But most of us just want to save the world.

Make way for a new generation.
We're hitting our prime in 2020—
An eye doctor's term for perfect vision.
Our parents' babes are now growing up
And we are responsible for precision.

Rebuilding the economic bust
With our own boom.
We're the one-of-a-kind batch
Littered with revealing tattoos
And student loan doom.

Sort out our resumes—
Class of 2011, 2012, 2013
Stacked with college degrees
But pushed aside
Due to "lack of experience"
As they say.
Our post-graduate Catch-22.

Make way for a new generation
America's glitter and glue.

Part Four

Quarantine

It's like we're all in a waiting room...
Checking a watch, checking the phone.
Eagerly holding on within our own.
It's a mystery of what's to come next,
Breaking News blaring on TV, in our texts.
The truth only told by doctors.
Visceral images of medical crews in distress,
Echoes of fear caving in
Self-diagnosing by taking a guess...
Drinking water, cup by cup
To pass the time until the day is up.
Holding our breath for a new beginning:
To exhale and venture out—
The bells will be ringing.

TV During Lockdown

Some will say
These recycled ads
Are just pushing pretentious fads
To milk the fat money,
Manipulate and milk your soul
If the search leads
Down a dark rabbit hole.

Pandemic Medical Workers

We must stay silent by HIPAA
But stress erupts louder
Than any bed alarm
Or ringing phone.
Dread snakes its way into
Morning huddle meetings.
All departments
All hands-on deck
And no hand touching
Foreign surfaces
In a building
Where we see life and death
Wrestling within the walls.
Temperatures, oxygen levels,
Shortness of breath.
"Positive" is now negative
"Negative" is now positive.
Reading the chart
Pierces the heart...
Gowns on, shields up
Pinch the gloves off
So delicately...
Return home
Throw the clothes off
Shower forever
Recharge the soul
Kiss the spouse
Warm up to the pet, child.
Read a book of leisure
Or a book of prayer.
We must stay silent, as we'll be told
Caring for young or old
From sunrise till the night is done...

But this virus
Will not silence
Optimism, Tenacity,
Ambition
For the sake
Of everyone.

Goodbye Through FaceTime

The pandemic stripped away all normalcy.
The hardest piece to pen down
Was nursing home family visits
Substituted by an iPad screen.

Weekly conversations clouded by confusion
Or mundane roadblocks of conversation
"What's new?"
"Nothing much going on here."

The hopeful hopelessness of saying "soon enough, we'll see you!"
As it stretches from days...
To weeks...
To months...
The echo of an adult child
Calling out to mom or dad, with little response.
Sudden release of forlorn dread,
Cooped up residents believing the unbelievable—
Exclamations of *"Get me out of the nuthouse!"*
Or
"Billy Joel songs are stuck in my head!"

Peruvian lilies, tulips, and veggie gardens
Put on display—the closest encounter to outdoors.
Sad news updates from families— like a dog passing.
Good news updates of pregnancies and due dates.

On an older woman's deathbed
I was assigned the call...
As she faded fast—
Her leg had been going gangrene.
The granddaughter took a call to read Psalms 100 and 103.
The older woman was never physically present
But present within the screen.
The family saw everything but
They weren't able to bid a farewell
Formally like in a traditional home—
No kin to hold her hand,
Nor any kisses on the forehead,
No tears fell on her skin,
None from the family...
But plenty of muted tears of my own.

Beagle

~Dedicated to Cora

Thin coat of fur, you pal around
My furniture and make the sound

"AROOO!"

When you really don't get your way
Or
When you see squirrels in our driveway.

You perch yourself on the bay window
A gaze into the horizon;
Glimpses of an unexpected bounty.

Certain sounds tickle your fancy—
The snap of a plastic sandwich container;
This you smell—bread and cheese involved,
You'll beg for titillating turkey!

Splotches of brown, and jet black.
White "booties" formed around paws...
I never want to send you back
To that secluded Susquehanna farm
Where we met each other's eyes
For the first time.

As a not-so-innocent pup,
You stole your brothers' sticks.
You also stole my heart.

One's First Child

As these lines come to form,
Poetry and parenthood
Likely
Had never been compared.

My baby, you will be
My most beautiful creation.
I must treasure every moment we share.

I must bring you a lot
Of nurture and care.
I know you will bring me
A lot of wear, tear, and prayer.

Time together cannot be measured nor predicted,
But the medley of life will play its part
In no particular order:

Music, Joy, Smiles, Falling Rain
Sunshine, Silence, and Tender Pain

The Colors of Wonder, Lively Play, and Tall Tales
Drinking, Dancing, Running Beyond Backyard Snails

Anger, Chores, Faith, Food
Arts, Crafts, and Tying Your Shoe

Kisses, Cries, Monday Groans
Messy Mistakes and Boo-Boo's on Bones

Changed Diapers, Broken Toys, and Frizzy Hair
Lessons Learned On What Is and Isn't Fair

Appointments, Play-Dates, Trips and Falls
Holidays, Parades, Grandparents, Soccer Balls...

I can write a book of poems,
But I cannot write the script set for your life.

Passion, growth, peace of mind
Will grace your soul as you may find.

July 2020: A Bob Dylan Lens

Millions of souls stuck at home—
So much uncertainty to harness.

Is there a loss in thriving
When you're surviving?
News reports become a bane
While boredom bargains with the rain.

You try not to think of death—
Coldest vapor calculation—
Swallowing you up like a whale
Into a tar mouth of devastation.

What is the darkest News?
Those that are jobless, some in seclusion,
Carrying daily anxiety
Battered and bruised.

Is the sword mightier than the pen?
Protests for policy, justice, social change—
A cultural reckoning and fusion.
So many more will plead to engage.

Lunch Regret

I should have added bacon—Story of my life.
I should have added bacon—Scrumptious spinach wrap was my plight.
I should have added bacon—The extra cost was $1.95!
I should have added bacon—Partly a reason to feel alive.
I should have added bacon—Fumbling through my wallet.
I should have added bacon—In the spur of the moment.
I should have added bacon—Such flavor and flair.
I should have added bacon—You were right there!

Hallmark Movies

Hallmark cozies up with my spouse
To sprinkle a new fairy tale in our house...

Staged desires, lukewarm conflicts
Middle class cuteness
Small town heart
Quirky dialogue, the near-miss kiss
From sudden feelings floating on screen.
The wealthy divorcée has a wise daughter.
A perky chef saves the café for her father.

Wedding bells chime
Fairy lights strung over rustic land
Awes of Christmas time
Then along comes some rogue "sturdy" man.

(As women hold their Friday wine)
They dream and playfully plan
Romantic or spontaneous gestures he may do
Like a carousel kiss or sailing under a sky so blue.

Remembering Rehoboth   ~For Kelly

It feels like we dreamed of the same dream
Within our own distant places.
Swept up in a cool breeze, the midst
Of a silent April night
Along the First State's finest beach—I first realized
That I fell in love with you.

It was not for sudden musings,
Nor the medicine
To shallow come and go's.

We simply embraced
A coastal ivory moon
Nestled serenely together
In a gazebo on Olive Avenue.

This moment—captured by lighthouse beam—
Felt like we were pinned forever,
Committed to the tender care
Love asks us to preserve
In an ageless dream.

Reverberate

I meditate to delineate
An endless universe where one must calculate
Any gliding speck that would fascinate
Our multitude of languages for the sake
Of a marvelous manifesto which can instigate
Symbolic tribes scattered among isles—triggering debate
On who holds the brilliant key to illuminate
Evocative words that can engineer a great
Revolution against the hopeless bends of a dark fate.
Step aside from the ironclad floodgate
Where ideas, passions, fears dwell and stagnate
As our principles and perceptions of love and hate
Duel in a vortex dimension—still at a stalemate
On how we as a species must operate.

Thanksgiving

What am I sincerely thankful for?
In a time of year when holiday commercialism teases us
To wish for more and more

Current society can be so fixated
About social media swag
That I can no longer
Feel the urge to humble-brag.

Thankfulness is so simple, a blessing in disguise.
To witness misfortunes of others, only seen by your eyes.

Never stacked upon your own shoulders. Not a dose.
Never burdened nor diagnosed.
Never stolen nor smeared.
Never fired, scammed, nor bullied.

Keep it all in clear view.
Dodging the distrust of another—
No thank you.

Thankfulness can do away these foul scents.
Thankfulness wholeheartedly is not a grand device—
Not the highest paying job
Nor the greatest hall or house
Even without the white picket fence.

Thankfulness is stitched in bondage
By a friend's advice
Or a family member's warm hug,
Maybe the dog smacking its lips.

Never should the pride hiding inside
All of us
Be nakedly overexposed.

Bravo to your baseball game tickets,
At least you have the money to pay.

Be thankful, not distasteful.

Pay attention to what others don't have.

Know limitations you're not dealt with day to day.

Know what's been taken and poor souls

Who got what was undeserved.

They'd run an Arctic mile
Just to have a reason to smile.

Eventually

Eventually—that worst-case scenario foe will hit a wall.
Eventually—that damn bench player's going to hit a ball.

Eventually—the right words will roll off your tongue.
Eventually—fortune's dusty bell will finally be rung.

Eventually—the ignorant Scrooge will give back.
Eventually—the addict will dispose of the pill pack.

Eventually—the truth about liars will be exposed.
Eventually—the right boss will keep you composed.

Eventually—the dazed firefighter catches up on his rest.
Eventually—the toddler will learn how to get dressed.

Eventually—the principled beggar will catch a fish.
Eventually—the head chef will craft his greatest dish.

Eventually—the imperfections won't feel as cruel.
Eventually—the promises of love will overrule.

Eventually—the great divide won't feel as wide.
Eventually—the moral compass will be your guide.

Eventually—the tide of faith grows greater than how it began.
Eventually—the world will change a little bit by your plan.

Current Human Conditions

~A series of Haiku

So clever and weird,
We cannot focus at all.
Nervous with no sense.

We will wash out pride
Reflect upon our conduct—
Study books inside

Or we will swerve out,
Selfishly demand ruin—
Ethics wane like drought.

Tasting purest thought,
We strive for natural gain
So art won't be lost.

Beyond the splendor
Humans must try purpose—
Bots are surrender.

Belief can form love
While devices simulate—
Speak truth all above!

February 13, 2022

~My take on the power of poetry

The keys to consciousness
The secret sauce of language
A declaration of history

A time capsule of imagination
An aura thermometer
Snapshots of space
The jukebox of actuality

The rich tableau of the soul
A love serum
A melody to madness
The emergency light to loss
A healing drumbeat
The echo of individuality

An emotional compass
A cathartic confession
The glowing embers of memory

The temple of truth
A mirror to mankind
The seed germinated for infinity

Love Letter to Lehigh Valley

Odyssey of the diesel emissions
Emitting from I-78
Under jets descending from the air
8 a.m. construction—vicious horns will blare.

Smoothly sip down
That Java Joint coffee
While cruising out of Trexlertown.

Cyclists steadily become friends
Blazing along the Velodrome bends.

Wineries spread out far and wide
Tucked along the hidden hills—
Many seen on the western side.

Blend in with the Crayola crowd.
Swing by Dorney to feed the ducks.
Carve out a lesson you learn
From Martin Guitars or Mack Trucks.

Pass by cornfields, trails, and some grand-standing warehouse
Or marvel at the Allentown "ArtsWalk" in your best blouse.

What would you want to do
After feeding giraffes at the zoo?
Stroll into Bethlehem Rose Garden before dark,
Listen to the Allentown Band's merry tunes from the park.

I get to the Sand Island Ice House,
Meet my "peeps" and a chatty guest
While muggy out-of-towners
Pack in party crowds at Musikfest.

Infinitely Pittsburgh

~Dedicated to fellow poet Chris Stipanovich.
Written in September of 2023. (Keep on writing!)

Mesmerized
By the rampant motion of a Yinz labeled yo-yo,
Coursing in all directions—
A speed of light spectacle
From a mysterious man
Standing against the promenade fountain.

You hear a clipper blare
Its nautical horn
Just off the edge of Station Square…

Gaze about this mountain-made
Urban ecosystem
Where three rivers converge
Along paths of cultured progress and heart—
A union of industry, athletics, and art.

Drive through the Fort Pitt tunnel—
Sit back and lower the sound.
Absorb the lights—take in the whole town.
The lucidity in your sense of wonder
Is unveiled to be a slice of sonder.

If Dementia Claims Me One Day

Moments slip away
From a bygone time
I may not spell right on paper,
Nor talk about coherently.

To my descendants,
I fear an unfathomable future
Years beyond this day.

I want you to keep
An unbreakable love
Forged from my legacy.

This may not be considered a crisp poem
That an artist may seek—
But a crystallization of my mind
While it is at its peak.

Be true to me, as I try to be
True to you.

The condition is unpredictable in
Handling, redirecting, appeasing
Bursts of tears, delusions and more...
Trying to walk so much
I may end up on the floor.

It is a mystery down the road
If I'll be with my darling wife
Or all alone.

Know that my purest passion
Involves watching sunsets outside—
A blissful practice when I go.
I'm uncertain down the line
If it'll be out a hazy window.

I want you to know
If my cognition fades,
Or if I have trouble sleeping at night
My heart will still have soil
With all its limited might.
So, please quench it fondly—
Keep my garden budding with life.

I won't see you every single day,
Especially if I am far away.
I will never want to feel like a hassle,
I don't wish to act like I own a castle.

I do not wish to be left entirely in the dark.
I'd rather not be the one
Stirring in bed while
People pass by
Staring at stylish phones,
Not caring
For these aching bones.

Please, I ask for no gossip or shame
Upon any such behaviors that I will not control
Whether I kick, spit, disrobe or stroll...
Expect any potential furniture stain.

I dread it deeply
If I will speak about
Things at random— ghastly or sexual.
Know that language and speech
May not be my strong suit.
I will still have an identity—
A smile, a sense for music,
A warmth for a furry animal!

One day— if I were to be next,
I will still possess a real soul.
Though nothing by 80 is conventional,
I dare not want to ever feel replaceable.

Keep Forever

~Dedicated to an older school aide who worked with me in one-to-one sessions (while I was in 2nd grade) to generate creative stories.

Will you ascribe value
To the roots of this holy vow?

Will you be the glorious actor
That takes a Broadway bow?

Will you pass on those dusty trophies
From tennis matches to the town fair—
To my most gracious kin?

Will you clear your throat
Then boldly declare
How you managed to win?

Will you help them preserve
Grandpa's sacred principle?

Will you carry over
Your wise-cracking wonder
To the well and back?

Will you seek the elder
White oak tree
Where you first kissed her
To engrave your names?

Will you find meaning
In every sweetest gaze?

Will you recall rhythmic waves
Holding you still
When her face
Radiated in the haze?

Will you confront the impossible
To paint life and see
All the ways

Clear and clever
On how you wished it would be?

Will you remember the days
That you want to keep forever?

The Next Phase In Our Existence

What will be our coming fate
When the next sight of comet Neowise
Zips down through an Earthly sky?
Destined for another 6,800 years
Humans must sit out and wait.

***

Restructured lands like Norway and Mexico
Collateral damage from quakes long ago
South Africa warped into an archipelago.
Fumes move past peaks near the rugged volcano,
All of what was lost from nearby Colorado.

Thunder eternally rumbles
But no visible creature stirs…
The oceans conquered over measured terrain
Trees vanished quicker from the acid rain.

Clocks all broken, salted by the freeze.
Deserts vastly blanket the scarce crust.
Skyscrapers succumbing to the seas.
Every last tombstone buried under dust.

***

I cannot manage nor see it all without being apocalyptic.
The end can arrive sooner or later, it's all so cryptic.
Skies drift by life and death, such a lengthy distance.
What will be the next phase in our existence?

About the Author

Thirty-five-year-old Brian Mahoney presents a second collection of poems in the book *Discovering Sea Glass*. His first book of poems titled *Uncommon Kaleidoscopes* was published back in 2011 by Aperture Press.

Brian graduated Kutztown University in 2012 with a Bachelor's Degree in Secondary Education (English). He eventually returned to school. He graduated from Lehigh Carbon Community College in 2019 with an Associate's Degree in the Occupational Therapy Assistant program.

Brian lives in the greater Lehigh Valley area with his wife, daughter, son, and dog.

Brian can be reached at brianmahoney213@gmail.com for questions or contact.